Dr Sellar has written more abou find in most of the commentar reflections come from a lifetime o pastoral and practical. Consequ Baptist's character and ministry are applied with a deceptive simplicity that can veil the wisdom of these brief expositions. The challenges to prayer are not intended to give easy answers, rather to stimulate those using this book to seek God's mind for themselves and so direct their prayers according to the Lord's will. Thus his succinctly brief petitions gently point readers to the way forward in their prayer lives. In the certainty that this book will be a source of blessing to the Lord's people, I am pleased to commend *The One Who Came Before*, knowing that, like the Baptist, it will guide them to 'Behold the Lamb of God, who takes away the sin of the world.'

David Searle
Former Pastor and Director of Rutherford House, Edinburgh
Author of several books

Frank Sellar is a pastor-teacher. This calling is clear on every page of his helpful series of daily studies on the life of John the Baptist. Each of the 31 studies includes a short summary of a passage drawn from the four gospels. This is supplemented with a question to ponder, showing the primary purpose of the book, which is for personal study and reflection. Finally there is a daily prayer which roots the study in the lived experience of the reader. The comments on the passage carefully take us back to the world of John and Jesus, asking the question, 'What did this text mean when it was first written?' While doing this, the writer then draws us forward in time to a 21st century world of domestic concerns and applications.

I am delighted to comment this helpful book to anyone seeking to read the Bible for themselves. You will benefit from the wise guidance of an experienced Bible teacher and pastor, and will re-discover the unfolding of God's big story of salvation, announced by the forerunner of the Messiah. Excellent!

David Bruce
Moderator of the General Assembly
The Presbyterian Church in Ireland

Here is a beautifully crafted introduction to a much neglected Biblical hero. It is rich in pastoral encouragement for believers under pressure, full of wise biblical insight for disciples living in an egocentric culture, and focused on prayerful application day by day. A devotional gem!

Jonathan Lamb
Author and Bible teacher, and minister-at-large
for Keswick Ministries

Frank Sellar's perceptive new devotional, *The One Who Came Before: 31 Days with John the Baptist*, will benefit all who read it with inspiring insights into John's life and calling. The author covers various complex issues with refreshing simplicity, issues like angelic appearances, and how to train our children in the Lord, and what genuine repentance looks like. Each devotion is short but satisfying, concluding with a penetrating question and prayer. Frank shows us how John consistently pointed others to Jesus, which is precisely what this devotional does! Read it – you will not only learn about John the Baptist, but your heart will resonate with John's words about Christ, 'He must increase, but I must decrease' (John 3:30).

Jani Ortlund
Author and speaker, Renewal Ministries, Nashville, Tennessee

John the Baptist's pivotal role in the fulfillment of God's promises in Christ can hardly be overstated, but we often just think of him as Jesus' relative or the man in strange clothes with an odd diet. In this book, Sellar takes readers through a series of daily reflections filled with biblical, theological, and practical insight that not only give John his due but, more importantly, are right in line with John's life and calling as a prophet pointing to Jesus who came to take away the sin of the world.

Brian Vickers
Professor of New Testament Interpretation and Biblical Theology, The Southern Baptist Theological Seminary, Louisville, Kentucky

Engaging, thoughtful and wise, Frank Sellar's 31-day devotional brings fresh eyes to a familiar story. Through bite-sized daily studies, he helps us to not only see John the Baptist more clearly, but also Jesus Christ, his Lord. Frank guides us verse by verse through each passage; explaining not just its meaning and original context; but how it applies to us today. He then closes with a short (but pithy) question and a suggested prayer. The great gift of this book is to encourage and challenge both our head and heart. It will bless all those who read it.

Emma Scrivener
Speaker and author of *A New Name* and *A New Day*

A fresh and thorough look at the extraordinary character of John the Baptist. But, even better than that, as you look at John you will find yourself marvelling at the greater One who came after him. Insightful, challenging and full of rich application. I thoroughly recommend it!

Jonty Allcock
Lead Pastor, The Globe Church, London

The
One
Who
Came
Before

31 Days With John the Baptist

Frank Sellar

CHRISTIAN
FOCUS

Copyright © Frank Sellar 2021

paperback ISBN 978-1-5271-0645-1
epub ISBN 978-1-5271-0749-6
mobi ISBN 978-1-5271-0750-2

Published in 2021
by
Christian Focus Publications Ltd,
Geanies House, Fearn, Ross-shire
IV20 1TW, Scotland
www.christianfocus.com

Cover design by Daniel van Straaten

Printed and bound by
Bell and Bain, Glasgow

Contents

Dedication
To the most significant person in my life, my wife
Claire, who thinks little about herself and much
about others.

How to use this book

This is an attempt to introduce you to someone really significant.

A person of whom Jesus Himself said, 'Among those born of women there has not risen anyone greater' (Matt. 11:11). Taking Bible passages about John the Baptist verse by verse, and making observations concerning what they say, what the text meant when first written and how it applies today, you are invited to dip into this last of the Old Testament prophets within the pages of the New Testament. And over one month (31 days) to better get to know someone even more important – the one he points us to – the Lord Jesus Christ!

Introduction

THE ONE WHO CAME BEFORE

Some while ago a very important person came to a service of worship at the congregation where I was minister. A short time before they arrived, a team of security personnel came to the building along with sniffer dogs and systematically cleared the way so that it was ready for the VIP.

Nothing in the history of planet earth could have been more important than the arrival of Messiah, the one spoken about, and eagerly anticipated, from the earliest chapters of the Bible (Gen. 3:15) to the very last book of the Old Testament (Mal. 4:5). The start of the Lord's ministry in space and time required preparation. It necessitated anticipation. The responsibility of doing that fell to a most unlikely individual.

UNCONVENTIONAL, COUNTERCULTURAL AND SELF-EFFACING

This leader's best indication of success was when people did not shine the light on himself, the warm-up performance, but instead focused on the main act. When men and women didn't applaud and adore him, but Jesus!

After 400 years of 'silence', that period of time between the Old and New Testaments during which Israel was ruled successively by the Medo-Persian Empire, the Greeks, Egyptians, Syrians and Romans, God communicated once again to the Jewish people – a resumption of the story of God's saving activity.

This book is an attempt to discover what the Gospel writers tell us about 'The one who came before', John the Baptiser, in his preparations for, and anticipation of, the arrival of the King of Kings and the Lord of Lords. Enjoy diving in!

The birth of John the Baptist foretold

The story begins with a baby. Or rather, without one, for Zechariah was old and Elizabeth his wife was menopausal. A house doesn't need a baby to be a happy home, but in days when children were seen as a reward from the Lord (Ps. 127:3-5) Elizabeth felt judged by other people (1:25).

At the time when Herod the Great was king of Judea, Zechariah was a priest in the Jewish Temple located in Jerusalem. There were some 8000 priests within 24 divisions of 300 men, and Zechariah served in Abijah's unit. He and his wife Elizabeth were upright in the Lord's eyes. Not sinless, but 'righteous in the sight of God' (v. 6). In other words, they were a praying couple seeking to live faithful and obedient lives.

One day when he was on duty, a 'lucky' thing happened to Zechariah. According to custom the presiding priest was chosen by lot and the lot fell on Zechariah to enter the Temple of the Lord, burn incense and offer prayers on behalf of the people. This opportunity did not come to every priest and it could only happen once in anyone's lifetime. It 'just so happened' to come Zechariah's way at this particular moment. 'The lot is cast into the lap, but its every decision is from the Lord' (Prov. 16:33). At this specific time, God chose to do something that would not only change Zechariah's life, but shape the course of history.

Back home, Elizabeth was not experiencing much luck. Just like many other godly women before her, she was unable to have children, and, being past natural child-bearing age, had no heir or offspring to take care of her or her husband in old age. Yet, despite bitter personal disappointment, she remained faithful, serving God.

Just as Zechariah placed the incense on the altar, representing the prayers of God's people, an angel – a messenger of the Lord – appeared to him. After reassuring Zechariah, God's messenger told the priest who he was and why he had come. 'Do not be afraid, Zechariah; your prayer has been heard. Your wife Elizabeth will bear you a son and you are to call him John' (v. 13).

It's a natural reaction to be alarmed when an angel of the Lord appears! Mary was afraid when she was told of Messiah's conception (Luke 1:30). The shepherds were filled with fear when they heard the news of Messiah's birth (Luke 2:10). The women were terrified when they met the angels announcing Christ's resurrection (Luke 24:5). But do not be shocked if God responds to the prayers of His people. God's purposes are furthered through this good news that astonishingly Elizabeth will have a baby and his parents will call him 'God is gracious' – 'John'.

'He will be filled with the Holy Spirit even before he is born'

John would be the source of joy both for his parents and for the whole community (v. 14). The angel reassured Zechariah that this boy would be 'great in the sight of the Lord' (v. 15).

Probably brought up as a Nazirite, according to the regulations of Numbers 6, John would be consecrated to the service of God under vows of abstinence from strong drink, letting his hair grow uncut and avoidance of contact with dead human bodies.

Instead of being filled with alcoholic spirits, John would be filled with the Holy Spirit even from his earliest moments. This would be his parents' joy and delight (v. 14), a picture of what would happen three decades later, on the Church's day of re-birth, 'Pentecost', when the Spirit would be poured out on all peoples.

'These people are not drunk, as you suppose,' said Peter, 'This is what was spoken by the prophet Joel: "In the last days, God says, I will pour out my Spirit on all people. Your sons and daughters will prophesy, your young men will see visions, your old men will dream dreams ... and everyone who calls on the name of the Lord will be saved"' (Acts 2:17-21).

Many parents are delighted at the birth of a baby. The deepest desire of most people, including many Christians, is that their child would be happy. But this is far too small a wish for those who trust in the Lord. As C.S. Lewis remarked in *God in the Dock*, even a bottle of Port can bring comfort! No one wants their offspring to have troubles in life, but believing parents can, and should, have much bigger desires than 'happiness' – that their children might be holy and useful in God's service.

Even as John was filled with the Holy Spirit from his earliest moments, Christian parents can pray that there might be no time that their children do not know and love the Lord Jesus for themselves. In this way, as they grow up within a context of trust and faith, their biggest delight will be to love and serve the Lord.

One of the greatest privileges of Christian parenthood is living in faith rather than fear for our children and for succeeding generations.

QUESTION
What's stopping me asking God for the infilling of God's Holy Spirit either for myself, members of my family or for others?

PRAYER
In your church community let's pray for children and parents: 'The LORD bless you and keep you; the LORD make his face shine on you and be gracious to you; the LORD turn his face toward you and give you peace' (Num. 6:24-26).

Day 3 Luke 1:18-25

Zechariah's silence

The angel finished speaking and Zechariah started talking. 'How can I be sure of this? I am an old man and my wife is well along in years' (v. 18).

Zechariah thought too little and spoke too quickly, so God gave him opportunity to stop talking and start listening. Nine months for wisdom to be implanted, grow and be born within his soul. We can be quick to tell God what to do rather than listen to what He says.

'I am Gabriel. I stand in the presence of God, and I have been sent to speak to you and to tell you this good news' (v. 19).

The angel who appeared to Zechariah while he was ministering in the Temple was none other than the Archangel, the Guardian of Israel, Gabriel, who had last appeared to Daniel (Dan. 8:16) and would shortly appear to Mary, announcing the birth of the Saviour (Luke 1:26). This was the highest possible delegation from the Lord to Zechariah, and yet while Daniel and Mary believed Gabriel's message, Zechariah didn't, because he was looking at his difficult circumstances rather than the Lord's character. And so, because of his lack of faith, it was no longer appropriate for one whose job it was to listen to and believe God's Word, to bring God's blessing to the people. He needed time out in order to learn to trust. Emerging from the holy place dumb, Zechariah struggled to communicate what had happened to him, so when his time of service was complete, he went home. This enforced sabbatical gave Zechariah opportunity to be renewed, and before long Elizabeth, his once barren, elderly wife, conceived!

Even as Sarah, Rebekah, Rachel, Hannah and Manoah's wives had biological infertility before God intervened in their lives and granted them a child, so now Elizabeth experienced tears of sadness before shedding tears of joy. The conception of a baby was appreciated all the more once the baby was born, a reminder that John was God's gift, not Zechariah and Elizabeth's by right, and that this child was lent to them as part of God's great purposes of grace.

QUESTION
How might I better listen to what God is saying to me today rather than talking to God?

PRAYER
Heavenly Father, forgive me if I live with a sense of entitlement; that somehow it is my right to expect certain things, rather than acknowledge that all I have is yours and everything that you grant to me is pure grace. Enable me please to be slow to speak and quick to listen, for Jesus' sake. Amen.

Nothing is impossible
with God

While Elizabeth and Zechariah were experiencing remarkable things in their southern context, Elizabeth's young cousin Mary and her fiancé Joseph were also encountering a life-changing event. God sent His chief messenger, the Archangel Gabriel, on a fresh expedition to Nazareth, a town in the northern region of Galilee, to indicate that God was going to bring about in Mary something that had never ever happened before. By the power of His Holy Spirit, none other than the Son of the Most High would be born, and He would be 'The Son of God' (v. 35).

In days before texting and Zoom, the angel revealed something special to the Virgin Mary: 'Even Elizabeth your relative is going to have a child in her old age, and she who was said to be unable to conceive is in her sixth month. For no word from God will ever fail' (v. 37). Elizabeth's pregnancy didn't just provide a loving companion for Mary, but tangible flesh and blood evidence and reassurance for Mary of what had been promised to her. Elizabeth's miracle had occurred several times before in Israel's history. Mary's virgin birth had never ever happened! Elizabeth's baby came as a result of a man and woman coming together. In Mary's case God was the father of her child. The roles of their babies were very different too. Elizabeth's baby would do what his dad should have done – fulfilled a priestly and prophetic role, preparing the way for the Lord; Mary's baby was that same Lord! The message from Gabriel to Mary was therefore even harder to believe and even more wonderful, so the Almighty gave Mary evidence that her baby would be who He is by providing Elizabeth as a visual aid that 'nothing is impossible for God'. Every time Mary questioned whether this was the Son of God in her womb, she could see old Elizabeth breastfeeding and be reminded that God's promises come true! Flesh and blood evidence of God's promises fulfilled.

QUESTION
What visual aids has God given me as reminders of His faithfulness?

PRAYER
Dear God, there are times in life when I just need someone else to talk to who understands. Enable me to be available for others requiring reassurance and, in my own fragility and vulnerability, please grant me renewed faith that all things are indeed possible with you. In Jesus' all-powerful name. Amen.

John's pre-natal response to Jesus

'I am the Lord's servant!' Mary answered the angel when she heard the news she was to bear the Son of the Most High, 'May your word to me be fulfilled.'

Unlike Zechariah who heard the angel and disbelieved, Mary trusted God, and hastily put a bag together and hurried to her cousin's home in the Judean countryside (v. 39).

She couldn't wait to see Elizabeth and share their mutual good news.

No sooner did they greet one another but the baby in Elizabeth's womb leapt for joy and Elizabeth was filled with the Holy Spirit. The same Holy Spirit who at creation inaugurated life (Gen. 1:2) and brought about the miracle of Mary's pregnancy with the Lord (v. 43), now did a work of grace in Elizabeth's life too, and in a loud voice Elizabeth exclaimed to her relative, 'Blessed are you among women and blessed is the child you will bear!'

A key mark of someone filled with the Holy Spirit of God is the desire to bless others and to adore the Saviour. Even as John himself was pointing to Jesus in the womb (as he would later in life), so now in her pregnancy John's mother did likewise and honoured the coming Christ.

Without pride or self-centredness, Mary and Elizabeth rejoiced in the goodness of God. They knew the reality of Nehemiah 8:10 that, 'the joy of the LORD is your strength.'

'Blessed is she who has believed that the Lord would fulfill his promises to her' (v. 45).

QUESTION

How might I go out of my way to bless someone today with words or deeds of encouragement?

PRAYER

Gracious God, thank you for the gift of the Saviour. I pray for those who find it difficult to have a child and for those who struggle to look after the children they have, and ask for them that any fears might be replaced by the calm miracle of His presence and purposes of grace in the power of the Holy Spirit. Amen.

John's birth and circumcision

The joy which John experienced as a Holy Spirit-filled pre-natal child now became the experience of Elizabeth's neighbours and relatives as well (v. 58).

On the eighth day it was the custom for a child of the covenant to be circumcised. For those within the household of faith it was a huge privilege for the next generation to be granted this sign and seal of God's grace. An indelible mark of belonging, cleansing, new life and God's call to obedience and trust.

The relatives came together for this naming ceremony where they assumed, in keeping with family tradition, that this infant would be called after his dad.

'Little Zec'. Not so! Elizabeth spoke up and said, 'No! He is to be called John.' This was God's choice, mediated by the angel (1:13) and when the puzzled neighbours turned to Zechariah for his opinion, he asked for his tablet and to everyone's astonishment wrote, 'His name is John.' This wasn't just a break in tradition, but a declaration that 'God is gracious'. This baby wouldn't so much have his dad's identity, but the Lord's!

Immediately Zechariah was freed up and enabled to do what he had been called to do. His mouth was opened and, just as on the Day of Pentecost when the Holy Spirit was poured out, Zechariah's tongue was loosed and he began to speak, praising God!

Months of silence had given this elderly priest opportunity to ponder, think and now testify and obey. Even good people can learn to trust deeper. Belief and obedience are vital for all who profess faith in God. Belief in theory is not enough. It requires experiential evidence.

Everyone who heard about this wondered about it, asking, 'What then is this child going to be?'

While the birth of any child is a miraculous thing, this was more. The birth and circumcision of this covenant child was a supernatural event ushering in the Messianic age: 'For the Lord's hand was with him' (v. 66).

QUESTION

Is there some tradition or thing in my background (even something good) I need to surrender to the Lord, freeing me for fresh, effective service?

PRAYER

Gracious Lord and loving heavenly Father, thank you for times of renewal and space-granting opportunity to ponder and then to act in obedience and faith. Enable me today not simply to believe with my head but to be obedient in my words and deeds giving honour to you, for Jesus' sake. Amen.

Zechariah's prophecy

The angel had promised that John would be filled with the Holy Spirit from his mother's womb (1:15). On meeting Mary who would bear the incarnate Lord, Elizabeth was also filled with the Holy Spirit (1:41). Now, having exercised obedience, Zechariah likewise was filled with the Spirit and prophesied words known to us as 'The Benedictus' (Blessed be the Lord God of Israel).

Far from this experience being a self-centred expression of paternal pride, under the Holy Spirit's prompting Zechariah spoke not so much about John, but about the one John would anticipate! In twelve verses, the initial eight speak of the Lord's redemption through the ages, from Abraham and David to the 'rising sun [who] will come to us from heaven to shine on those living in darkness and in the shadow of death' (vv. 78-79).

Yes, John will be called a 'Prophet of the Most High' (v. 76), but his role will not be to draw attention to himself, but to point to the one who would 'give his people the knowledge of salvation through the forgiveness of their sins' (v. 77).

Zechariah, filled with the Spirit of God, acknowledged the Lord is not remote and far away, but one who draws near and cares. And that their greatest joy is to anticipate a new Exodus, whereby the people of God might be rescued from the hands of their enemies and granted the freedom to love and serve without fear of destruction or oppression.

What is the greatest prayer any parent can offer on behalf of their children?

Pleasure? Safety? Self-fulfilment and confidence? Sadly, believing parents may limit themselves to only wishing for their kids small things, no different from non-Christians! Guided by the Holy Spirit, Zechariah yearned that his son's number-one passion might be to point people to Jesus, and that his child's greatest fulfilment would be in magnifying the one who grants light to those who sit in darkness and comes to the rescue of His people. This can be our large prayer too, for our children and for young people within the church family.

QUESTION
How might I pray for my children, grandchildren, nieces, nephews or friends BIG prayers of faith?

PRAYER
Gracious God, forgive me when my prayers for others are far too introverted, self-centred and comfortable. Please grant me a larger vision of your great purposes of redemption so that I, the children around me and members of the church community, might point to Jesus the rescuer and giver of life. Amen.

John's preparation

'And the child grew and became strong in spirit; and he lived in the wilderness until he appeared publicly to Israel' (v. 80).

One verse describes thirty years of John's life. His parents played their part.

Elizabeth and Zechariah had prayed for him. They had thanked God for him and sought the Holy Spirit's blessing upon him. They had loved, nurtured and cared for him physically, emotionally and spiritually. A parent's role in raising their children is fundamental for behavioural stability, adjustment, and wellbeing.

Just as no mum or dad would leave the responsibility for feeding their child to neighbours, no worthy parent should abdicate the privilege of training their child spiritually. It is a Christian parent's fundamental duty to lead, guide and shape their children and teenagers in the nurture and admonition of the Lord, so that they grow up in the knowledge and love of the Saviour. 'Start children off in the way they should go, and even when they are old they will not turn from it' (Prov. 22:6).

A parent's responsibility lessens when their offspring flies the nest, with the increasing prayer that 'The one who began a good work in [them] will carry it on to completion until the day of Christ Jesus' (Phil. 1:6).

It is often only when children leave the safety and confines of the home that their parents discover if they own the Christian faith for themselves and seek the company of others within whom the Holy Spirit also dwells.

Even as Israel had spent time in the wilderness before coming through the Jordan into the Promised Land, so now John lived in the desert prior to engaging in his baptising ministry beside that very same river. There he spent time with God, growing in faith and knowledge of the Scriptures before ministering to others. There he spent time seeking God's purpose for his life rather than hoping that God might fit into his.

QUESTION

If I have children in my life how can I best train them in knowing the Saviour through the Scriptures?

PRAYER

Heavenly Father, thank-you so much for those who encouraged me in my faith growing up. I long that my children and the younger generation would own the faith into which they were nurtured. Grant them the infilling of the Holy Spirit to enable them to love you supremely and so face the temptations of flesh, the world and the devil. And for any who have wandered away, please draw them back to yourself and into useful service, for Jesus' sake. Amen.

And so John came

Mark's Gospel tells us John came baptising in the desert region and preaching a baptism of repentance for the forgiveness of sins. Immediately prior to this, Mark quotes from two Old Testament prophets, Malachi and Isaiah:

'I will send my messenger, who will prepare the way before me' (Mal. 3:1).

'A voice of one calling: In the wilderness prepare the way for the Lord; make straight in the desert a highway for our God' (Isa. 40:3).

Malachi is the final prophet quoted in our Old Testament. He was writing to Israel at a time when oppressive Persians were dominating their land. The people were expecting God to vindicate them. Instead, Malachi declared that while the Lord will indeed come, He will come not to judge the wicked foreigners but His own people, removing their dross and making them pure so that they may be of greater value. 'He will be like a refiner's fire or a launderer's soap ... He will purify the Levites and refine them like gold and silver' (Mal. 3:2-3).

Mark tells us, and Jesus confirms, that John the Baptist was the one about whom this was written (Matt. 3:1-3). He was the outrider going before the monarch's entourage to clear the route the Messiah would take, making the path straight and preparing hearts to encounter the King.

Likewise, Isaiah the Prophet, speaking even earlier than Malachi says:

'Prepare for God's arrival! Make the road straight and smooth, a highway fit for our God. Fill in the valleys, level off the hills, smooth out the ruts, clear out the rocks. Then GOD's bright glory will shine and everyone will see it. Yes. Just as God has said' (Isa. 40:3-5, MSG).

John was that envoy. The one with blue flashing lights indicating that someone of great significance was about to arrive in order to judge and redeem. And so, John came urgently calling people to turn to God and to be washed and made clean from all the filth and dirt in their lives in anticipation of meeting the King.

QUESTION
What obstacles and unhelpful things do I need to ask God to help me get rid of in my life so that I am ready for usefulness in His service?

PRAYER
'Let every heart be cleansed from sin.
Make straight the way for God within.
And so prepare to be the home
Where such a mighty guest may come.'[1]

---

1. 'On Jordan's bank'. Original by Charles Coffin 1676-1749. Adapted by Michael Perry 1942-96.

John's popularity

'The whole Judean countryside and all the people of Jerusalem went out to him.'

News of John spread quickly and, just as the peoples of Isaiah and Malachi's day heard their prophetic words, so people of John's day were intrigued by his compelling and unconventional communication. Unlike the Sadducean and Pharisaical leaders who appeared sectarian, predictable and institutionalised, here was a charismatic figure who had a powerful message to proclaim and a passion to match.

The location of John's ministry is significant, and not just because it was prophesied by Isaiah. In the book of Exodus the wilderness was the place where God guided, spoke to, and walked with His people before entering the promised destination, the land of rest. The desert was a place of fresh opportunities.

John's location then, was a situation of desolation, but also a context of new hope.

Like the prophets before him, John knew that renewal required repentance.

'Confessing their sins, they were baptised by him in the Jordan River.'

He was not saying that a dip in water was sufficient to bring about forgiveness, but washing was a potent visual aid that indicated a desire to move over from a place of alienation into a right relationship with God who is altogether pure and clean and holy.

This was a startling call, since ablution was a requirement for Gentiles who wished to convert to Judaism. John was implying that those who think of themselves as 'chosen' were in fact no different to outsiders! They too, like the Children of Israel centuries before, passing through the water from the place of slavery to freedom, required a wake-up call to repentance and new life in clean, fresh water. All of them needed to leave behind lives of sin, rebellion and slavery, represented by Egypt, and set their sights on the place of obedience, faith and trust in the Promised Land of God's shalom.

QUESTION
Are there things that I am particularly proud of in my background that are actually preventing me from discerning my true spiritual needs?

PRAYER
Heavenly Father, I long to be renewed, but too often I also want to hold on to the sinful idols of my heart that are harmful for effective spiritual growth and development. Point out to me attitudes and actions that need to be turned away from, so that I may serve you freely without hindrance, for Jesus' sake. Amen.

'After me comes the one more powerful than I'

Elijah had ministered in the region of the Jordan and likewise John's attire fitted both the location and tradition of this ninth-century B.C. prophet.

Dressed in camel's hair with a leather belt, John ate locusts and wild honey.

Just as Malachi had declared that an Elijah-like figure would precede the day of the Lord (Mal. 3:1 and 4:5) so John adopted Elijah's distinctive clothing (2 Kings 1:8) as a visual aid of the prophetic message which he proclaimed:

'After me comes the one more powerful than I, the straps of whose sandals I am not worthy to stoop down and untie. I baptise you with water, but he will baptise you with the Holy Spirit' (v. 7-8).

If the location and dress of John was unconventional, his message was countercultural: Don't look at me – look out for the one who will come after me!

I'm not even worthy enough to act as a slave tasked with unbuckling the shoes of the one who will follow me. I baptise with something purely physical. He will baptise with something (or rather someone) profoundly spiritual, God's very own Holy Spirit. (Matthew and Luke add 'and with fire'.)

Even as, centuries before, the Children of Israel had come through the waters of the Red Sea and travelled through the wilderness accompanied by pillars of cloud and fire, so now, having experienced the first (water) in John's baptism, they could reasonably anticipate the second (fire) also.

In fulfilment of what the prophets Isaiah (Isa. 32:15), Ezekiel (Ezek. 36:26-27) and Joel (Joel 2:29-32) had said, God would make His presence felt both personally and powerfully.

On the Day of Pentecost (Acts 2:2-4) following Christ's ministry, death, resurrection and ascension, this became the living and active experience of the fragile, discouraged followers of Jesus, enabling them to be equipped and enabled to go into all the world and proclaim the message of the gospel, whatever the cost.

As we face all the challenges today brings, we do so only in the Spirit's strength.

QUESTION

How might I point someone to Jesus as the altogether powerful one today?

PRAYER

'Guide me O my Great Redeemer,
Pilgrim through this barren land.
I am weak, but you are mighty.
Hold me with your powerful hand.'

(William Williams, 1745)

A witness to the light

In John's Gospel, we encounter John the Baptist as a man who was 'sent **from** God' (v. 6) – a witness to the one who was in the beginning **with** God and who **is** God. John, the sent one, was not himself the light, but someone who prepared people to look out for the bright, clear and shining light.

'He who comes after me has surpassed me because he was before me,' said John the Baptist (v. 15). Just like a best man who looks out for, cares for and magnifies the bridegroom (John 3:28-29), so John recognised his purpose and his delight was to glorify the one who was far superior to him and existed before him, not pushing himself forward but honouring Christ Jesus. All of us have been to weddings where the best man has spoken more about himself than the groom or even poked fun at or mocked him, and we have cringed.

John's light (John 5:35) was not a spotlight focused on himself, but one which projected onto the central character on the stage of world history – the Bridegroom who is the 'true light who gives light to everyone' and has come to love and rescue His beloved bride, the Church.

Those who win people to themselves rather than Christ fail both themselves and the Lord. Those who win people to Christ rather than themselves, gain both.

QUESTION

How might being Christ's bride change the way I act toward Jesus and His church today?

PRAYER

Heavenly Father, thank you for Jesus, the most perfect and wonderful self-revelation of yourself. I bless you that I do not have to search around in the dark looking for you, but you have come searching for me in the person of your only beloved Son. Amen.

Jesus' baptism by John

'Then Jesus came from Galilee to the Jordan to be baptised by John' (3:13).

Having first met prenatally thirty years earlier when Elizabeth and Mary talked excitedly of God's purposes of grace, now the long-anticipated Messiah steps onto the scene, and His first act was to be baptised by John in the Jordan River!

What a peculiar thing! The one who had His own personal outrider preparing the way for His arrival, now appears, says nothing, and instead submits to a plunge into water just like countless others!

Surely Jesus ought to be the one who washes me? At least that's what John thought. Jesus had no need to be baptised for forgiveness because He was sinless (2 Cor. 5:21 and Heb. 4:15). Yet in His desire to identify with sinful humanity and in order to stand alongside John and to affirm his message, in the words of Isaiah 700 years earlier, 'He was numbered with the transgressors, for he bore the sin of many' (Isa. 53:12). As Glen Scrivener has phrased it, 'Jesus joined us in our filth so we could join him in his family.' In spite of John's protest, (3:14), John consented, and as soon as Jesus came up out of the water, He saw heaven being torn open and the Spirit descend upon Him like a dove. Just as in Song of Songs the dove symbolised loving innocence, so now the Holy Spirit descended upon Jesus, and in an echo of Genesis 22 where Abraham took his son, his only son Isaac, and was prepared to offer him as a sacrifice, now a voice came from heaven saying, 'This is my Son, whom I love; with him I am well pleased.' At this moment of triune holiness, Jesus was set apart from all other prophets, priests or kings before Him and affirmed by the Father as God's unique, beloved Son and anointed by the Spirit for the unparalleled task ahead of Him as the sacrificial Saviour of the world.

Having accepted this affirmation, Matthew tells us that straight from the Jordan, Jesus was led by the Spirit into the desert to be tested by the devil. Immediately from the waters of life He experienced a forty-day trial in the barrenness of the wilderness. Would Jesus, God's Son, be able to achieve there what Israel failed to do during their forty years in the desert?

QUESTION

Are there times I have experienced severe testing immediately following great blessing?

PRAYER

Heavenly Father, thank you that Jesus plumbed the depths of my disgrace so that I wouldn't have to. Thank you that He triumphed where all others before Him had failed. Enable me please to fight the temptations of Satan not by might, not by power, but by Christ's Spirit. Amen.

'I am not the Christ'

John the Baptist's preaching caused such a stir that a delegation was sent from Jerusalem to establish his identity. John as a truthful, transparent prophet knew his purpose was not to create fake news nor arouse wrong expectations of himself, so when the priests and Levites asked him who he was, 'He did not fail to confess, but confessed freely, "I am not the Messiah"' (v. 19). In those days, many Jewish people were looking for Messiah – a revolutionary figure anticipated to lead rebellion against the occupying Roman forces. John insisted he was not the Anointed One; his role was merely giving testimony to the one soon to be revealed.

Next they asked 'Elijah?'

He said, 'I am not.'

'Are you the Prophet?' (a new Moses)

'No.'

Finally they said, 'Who are you? Give us an answer to take back to those who sent us.'

Replying using the words of Isaiah the prophet, he said 'I am the voice of one calling in the desert, "Make straight the way for the Lord."'

Three negatives: 'Not, Not, No'!

One positive.

'I am a voice.'

John was a faithful preacher. A humble herald, speaking, calling, warning people to look out for, and get ready for, the King. His task was not to be clever, smart or entertaining. His role was not to focus on himself but his sole purpose was to be heard and not seen!

Later in John's Gospel we read of another delegation; this time to Jesus' disciple Philip:

'Sir,' they said. 'We would like to see Jesus' (John 12:21).

QUESTION
Are there times I am tempted to 'massage the facts' or give an impression of myself that is less than totally honest?

PRAYER
'What gift of grace is Jesus my Redeemer
There is no more for heaven now to give
He is my joy, my righteousness, and freedom
My steadfast love, my deep and boundless peace
To this I hold, my hope is only Jesus
For my life is wholly bound to His
Oh how strange and divine, I can sing: all is mine!
Yet not I, but through Christ in me.'[1]

---

1. 'Yet not I, but through Christ in me', Michael Ray Farren, Richard C. Thompson, Jonny Robinson, CityAlight, 2018.

Day 15 *Matthew 11:7-14; John 1:19-20*

Was John the Baptist
Elijah or not?

John the Baptist was swift to deny that he was the Prophet Elijah (John 1:21).

Elijah hadn't been reincarnated! John identified himself as simply a humble herald, giving testimony to the Messiah soon to be revealed before the great and terrible day of the Lord.

Yet, in Matthew 11:14 Jesus declared that for those ready to accept it, John was the Elijah who was to come. How are we to understand this apparent conundrum?

Luke 1:17 gives the clue when it makes clear that John came 'in the spirit and power' of Elijah. John was not Elijah in a literal sense. John was the fiery New Testament forerunner who points the way to the arrival of the Lord Jesus, just as Elijah fulfilled that mighty role in the Old Testament.

Even as Elijah spoke strongly against the sin in peoples' lives, and was associated with the fire of God's judgment on idolatry, and was hated and pursued by the political powers of his generation, so John, who appeared at this critical moment of history, was forthright in his words and call to repentance.

He too confronted and was rejected by both political and religious leaders of his day.

He also dwelt in the desert and ate a primitive diet like his predecessor (1 Kings 17:6 and Matt. 3:4).

46

Both were the victims of malicious women: Jezebel (1 Kings 19:2) and Herodias (Matt. 14:6-10) who sought to kill God's messenger rather than listen to God's message.

Both Elijah and John awakened people to spiritual and moral responsibilities and, as prophets of the Most High God, tasked and enabled by the Spirit, they did not speak their own words but articulated a message from the Lord to all who had ears to hear.

Some people become disquieted because the preacher at church highlights issues from the Scriptures that are both inconvenient and disconcerting. But where else can followers of the Lord Jesus have their minds challenged and measured against Christ's standard and be encouraged to live faithful, holy and just lives? Give thanks for dedicated ministers who, like skilful surgeons wielding the sharp knife of God's Word, identify and excise sin so that the entire body may remain healthy and active.

QUESTION

How best can I pray for my pastor or church leaders in their responsibility to be faithful proclaimers of the Word of God?

PRAYER

Thank you for unwavering ministers of the gospel who take their responsibility seriously, and their authority from the Scriptures and not from popular opinion. Help me to submit to what I hear as from yourself and enable me each day to live a life of repentance for the sake of Jesus the obedient Son. Amen.

'Behold the Lamb of God'

The next day John saw Jesus coming towards him and said, "Look, the Lamb of God, who takes away the sin of the world!"'

Using his voice – the voice God had given him, John encouraged those who had been looking at him to gaze in another direction – and see a lamb!

Students of art history will be familiar with artists who have sought to depict this scene. Leonardo da Vinci, Albrecht Durer and Titian to name a few.

John the Baptist situated to one side of the canvas – pointing away from himself and enabling people to behold the central character of the scene, Jesus.

'Lamb of God' is an unusual title for any human being, but the Jewish people would have been familiar with the lamb as a symbol of sacrifice, freedom and salvation.

In Genesis 22 as the Patriarch Abraham piled the wood on the back of his beloved son, his only son whom he loved, and struggled up Mt Moriah to the place of potential sacrifice, Isaac spoke up and said to his father, 'The fire and the wood are here, but where is the lamb for the burnt offering?' and Abraham replied, 'God himself will provide the Lamb.'

In Exodus 12, as the children of Israel planned to depart from the place of slavery in Egypt and flee to their promised rest they were urged to take a lamb and kill it, sprinkling its blood on the sides and tops of the door frames:

'And when I see the blood, I will pass over you. No destructive plague will touch you when I strike Egypt' (Exod. 12:13).

And in Isaiah chapter 53:4-7, as the Prophet spoke 700 years before Christ of the 'Suffering Servant', there is a description of a lamb led to the slaughter:

'Surely he took up our pain and bore our suffering, yet we considered him punished by God, stricken by him, and afflicted. But he was pierced for our transgressions, he was crushed for our iniquities; the punishment that brought us peace was on him , and by his wounds we are healed.'

'Look', said John. 'Here is the ultimate, totally sufficient sacrificial Lamb of God.'

John the Divine later writes: 'With your blood you purchased for God persons from every tribe and language and people and nation ... Worthy is the Lamb who was slain, to receive power and wealth and wisdom and strength and honour and glory and praise!' (Rev. 5:9-11).

QUESTION
Even as artists and songwriters have used their talents to enable people to behold Jesus, how might I use my gifts to do likewise?

PRAYER

'Taking my sin, my cross, my shame
Rising again I bless Your name
You are my all in all
When I fall down You pick me up
When I am dry You fill my cup
You are my all in all.
Jesus, Lamb of God
Worthy is Your name'[1]

---

1. 'You are my all in all', Dennis Jernigan, 1992.

'He must become greater. I must become less.'

As Jesus' light became brighter, John was content to permit the spotlight to shine on the bridegroom, for 'whoever lives by the truth comes into the light' (v. 21).

As Jesus gathered a group of followers around Him and discipled them, John continued to baptise at a place called Aenon near Salin, because there was plenty of water there and people were still coming to him to be baptised. With both John and the disciples of Jesus practising ceremonial washing in the same region, onlookers and their own followers were beginning to get confused about their relative significance. Soon a vigorous argument was going on and John's disciples came to John and said: 'Rabbi, that man who was with you on the other side of the Jordan – the one you testified about – well, he is baptising and everybody is going to him!' (v. 26).

This gave John the opportunity to speak of Jesus' supremacy over all as he replied, 'A person can receive only what is given them from heaven. You yourself can testify that I said: "I am not the Messiah but am sent ahead of him." The bride belongs to the bridegroom. The friend who attends the bridegroom waits and listens for him, and is full of joy when he hears the bridegroom's voice. That joy is mine, and it is now complete. He must become greater. I must become less' (John 3:27-30).

Since Jesus was God's chosen one, the Lamb of God (1:23-34), there really was no competition between himself and Christ. God had entrusted each with particular responsibility, and John's delight was to enjoy Jesus' supremacy. He was not a perfect man, but he was a perfect witness.

In his humble acceptance of, and delight in, his God-given role and responsibilities, John is a beautiful example for all disciples to follow. Even after faithful service he never started to think that he 'deserved' any acknowledgment for himself. His sole mission was to see people focus their attention on the Lord Jesus. In the Christian Church there is no place for competition, self-seeking, jealousy or rivalry. The believer's goal is to see Christ and His Kingdom develop, thrive and flourish. 'I must decrease. Jesus must increase.'

QUESTION
What parts of me are centerstage rather than Jesus? How might I become less important and Jesus even more significant?

PRAYER
Heavenly Father, I pray for members and leaders in my church fellowship in their various roles and callings and ask you to bless them as they serve for the benefit of the entire body. I also pray for other congregations that seem to be thriving better than our own. May they know of our genuine love and prayers and ask that their efforts to win many for Christ might be rewarded, for His glory. Amen.

'Produce fruit in keeping with repentance'

John's location was strange (the desert in Judea).
John's diet was strange (locusts and wild honey).
John's clothing was strange (camel's hair and leather belt).
John's preaching was strange (repentance).

'When he saw many of the Pharisees and Sadducees coming to where he was baptising, he said to them, "You brood of vipers! Who warned you to flee from the coming wrath? Produce fruit in keeping with repentance"' (Matt. 3:7-8).

This was an odd message! No comforting words or moralistic sentiments. No attempt to win friends or influence people, but a full-frontal attack on the political and religious leaders of his day. These were people who were meant to lead others in the way of righteousness. Instead they had relied on their own status and ethnicity for their standing and position in society and failed to live faithful, fruitful lives. In spite of their privileged position, John said they were under the judgment of God. Just as snakes slither away from a burning bush under which they have been hiding, these fork-tongued leaders would not escape the fire (v. 10).

It is a brave preacher who is prepared to call the leaders of church and state to repent. To turn around. To be converted and to have a change of mind. This forthrightness would eventually lead to John's own execution.

The Apostle Paul, himself not a stranger to suffering for preaching God's truth, urged the Christians in Rome not to be conformed to the patterns of secular society but rather to be transformed by the renewing of their minds (Rom. 12:2).

Behaviour follows belief, and both John and Paul argued that God's Kingdom demands a radical redirection of life away from sin and self and towards Christ Jesus who is the judge (Acts 10:42).

QUESTION

Where might my pressure points be to 'fit in' rather than 'stand out' today?

PRAYER

'Legalistic remorse says, "I broke God's rules", while real repentance says, "I broke God's heart".'[1] (Timothy Keller)

Heavenly Father, please enable me, out of a true sense of my sin and an awareness of your great mercy in Christ, to turn from all my evil and wrongdoing toward yourself with grief and hatred of the many ways I have hurt you. May it lead to a fresh obedience for Jesus' sake. Amen.

---

1. Timothy Keller, *The Church Planter Manual,* (Redeemer Presbyterian Church), 2002.

John's practical teaching

So then, what does a renewed mind look like in practice? People in John's day weren't satisfied with generalities. They wanted down-to-earth guidance as to what repentance might mean for them. '*What should we do then?*' the crowd asked. John answered, 'Anyone who has two shirts should share with the one who has none, and anyone who has food should do the same' (v. 11).

Repentant people can't be selfish, greedy or uncaring. Repentant people must be generous, compassionate and charitable, because God has been kind and gracious to us. Tax collectors also came to be baptised. '*Teacher, what should we do?*' 'Don't collect any more than you are required to,' he told them (v. 13).

Repentant people can't be dishonest because God is just.

Then some soldiers asked him, '*And what should we do?*' John replied, 'Don't extort money and don't accuse people falsely – be content with your pay' (v. 14).

Repentant people can't be grasping, abusive or corrupt. They must be respectful, fair and impartial because God loves integrity and hates bribes (Ps. 26:6-12).

Here is straightforward teaching about what faith looks like in practice. People shaped by the Spirit of God will be gracious, honest, just and content.

Years before John, the prophet Micah put it this way, 'He has shown you, O mortal, what is good. And what does the Lord require of you? To act justly and to love mercy and to walk humbly with your God' (Micah 6:8).

A call to repentance is not merely an invitation to have Jesus as Saviour, but as LORD over every aspect of life.

Spirituality is more than going to church, praying, getting baptised and attending communion, vital as these excellent things are. Christian faith is living in a right relationship with God and with people made in His image.

In a world where there is huge disparity between rich and poor, prejudice toward people of other religions, colours, backgrounds and opinions, Christian people must be different from those who profess no faith in Jesus.

The Apostle James put it this way, 'What good is it, my brother and sisters, if a person claims to have faith but has no deeds? Can such faith save him? Suppose a brother or sister is without clothes and daily food. If one of you says to them, "Go, I wish you well, keep warm and well fed", but does nothing about their physical needs, what good is it? In the same way, faith by itself, if it is not accompanied by action, is dead' (James 2:14-17).

QUESTION
Well? What do I need to do right now in obedient response?

PRAYER

Heavenly Father, as a kind and holy God you call us to lives of integrity and generosity. Show me today what this looks like practically at school, college, work or home and make me discontent if I live selfishly in the face of others' great need. In Jesus' disconcerting but liberating name. Amen.

'He will baptise you with the Holy Spirit and with fire'

With such strong and powerful teaching, people were waiting expectantly and were wondering in their hearts if John might possibly be the Messiah.

'John answered them all, "I baptise you with water. But one who is more powerful that I will come, the straps of whose sandals I am not worthy to untie. He will baptise you with the Holy Spirit and with fire. His winnowing fork in his hand to clear the threshing floor and to gather the wheat into his barn, but he will burn up the chaff with unquenchable fire." And with many other words John exhorted the people and preached the good news to them' (vv. 16-18).

To the modern mind a message of refining, purification and judgment is hardly 'good news' because it jars with our sensibilities about tolerance. But surely every person yearns that suffering be reversed, injustices corrected, and wrongs rectified?

The good news preached by John is that Jesus will one day make every bad thing good and that in doing so, as the sin-bearing Holy Spirit-baptising Messiah, He would take all that judgment we deserved on Himself.

Whatever your experience of injustice, hurt or pain, wickedness will not have the final say.

Day 21 Luke 3:19-20

Herod's response to
John's preaching

John's message was not 'good news' for Herod Antipas.

His preaching about 'sifting', 'purifying' and 'judging' wasn't received favourably by the ruler Jesus called 'that Fox'. The Tetrarch of Galilee and Perea regarded it his role – not John's, to decide what was right and wrong – particularly in regards to his sex life. The Jewish historian Josephus provides some background that the Bible doesn't mention. Early in his reign, Antipas was married to the daughter of King Aretas of Petra. However, on a visit to Rome he had stayed at the home of his half-brother Herod II and there he fell in lust with his wife Herodias. The two agreed to marry after Antipas divorced. John attacked the adulterous and incestuous marriage, as Herodias was also Antipas's niece, a clear violation of Levitical purity laws, and criticised him for many other evil things that he had done.

This did not go down at all well with Herod's new wife and so Antipas locked John up in the prison of his Dead Sea palace at Machaerus, supposing that by doing so, he would no longer be troubled by this tiresome preacher or by his message of 'looking to the Lamb', but thereby adding yet another wicked thing to his catalogue of sins.

John's message of repentance – preparing the way for the teaching of Jesus – brought social, moral and political implications.

Christians believe the Scriptures have vital connections both on matters of personal morality and also in the public square. Where believers live according to Bible standards, or challenge either the unethical behaviour of political or religious leaders, or criticise legislative or societal injustices, they open themselves up to the inevitability of criticism, cancelling, ridicule and even punitive consequences.

Indifference to social sins of corruption, exploitation, hunger, environmental issues, climate change, pornography, abortion, sexual immorality, violence against women, sectarianism, racism, bonded labour and sex slavery is not an option for the believer filled with the Holy Spirit. Christian people must share the heart and passion of the one who is altogether holy, and sifts and purifies and judges rightly.

QUESTION

I can't do everything, but I can do something. Which one issue ought I to get involved with?

PRAYER

Dear God, please give courage to Christians to recognise the injustices and wrongs of society and, in humility, grant wisdom to know how most effectively to address such issues with selflessness. I pray for churches and organisations dedicated to making a difference to the common good, in spite of huge pressures to do nothing, in Jesus' name. Amen.

'Teach us to pray'

'One day Jesus was praying in a certain place. When he had finished, one of his disciples said to him, "Lord, teach us to pray, just as John taught his disciples."'

It is thanks to John the Baptist that Christians have what we call 'The Lord's Prayer'. Having observed Jesus praying, it was so compelling that a follower yearned to know how to pray himself. Having perhaps known one of John's disciples and being aware that he had instructed his disciples to pray, Jesus' disciple was motivated to ask for similar instruction.

Praying, then, was clearly part of John the Baptist's life.

Familiar as he was with the Scriptures – what we know as the Old Testament – he would have been familiar with great prayers of the Bible such as:

Moses' prayer of praise (Exod. 15:1-18).

Hannah's prayer of adoration (1 Sam. 2:1-10).

Jonah's prayer of salvation (Jonah 2:2-9).

David's prayer of deliverance (Ps. 3).

He would have used prayers such as these as models or examples for himself and his disciples to emulate and make their own.

Praying was something John felt was important to teach his disciples. He did not assume they would know how to pray without instruction. Praying clearly shaped the

Lord Jesus' life so deeply, and John's life before Him, that it was something their disciples wanted to experience for themselves because it was so living and attractive.

Jesus said, 'When you pray'. Not 'if'. And when you pray 'Say Abba, dear Father.'

Prayer is relational.

'Hallowed be your Name.' While God is Father, He is also holy, and to be revered.

'Your Kingdom come.' We look forward to the day when God's rule will be experienced all over the world.

'Give us each day our daily bread.' Just as the Hebrews were provided with manna in the wilderness each morning, please grant us sufficient for our needs, keeping us humbly dependent.

'Forgive us our sins as we forgive everyone who sins against us.' As we have been wonderfully forgiven at great cost to yourself, grant us forgiving spirits toward others also.

'And lead us not into temptation.' May we avoid wrongdoing which would harm our relationship with you, weaken our faith or make us ineffective in service.

And this we pray in Jesus' name. Amen.

QUESTION
What steps can I take to pray more faithfully and biblically?

PRAYER
Dear Heavenly Father, through the gift of prayer, please align me nearer to your will, rather than me wanting yours to bend to mine. For Jesus's glory. Amen.

'Are you the one to come?'

By now Jesus was well established. He was well known in the region and His preaching and healing ministry was gaining momentum. John's disciples heard about Jesus' teaching, miracles and discipleship training (Matthew 5–7, The Sermon on the Mount) and told John about it in prison. Locked up in Herod's jail, John had his momentary doubts. Calling two, he sent them to the Lord to ask, 'Are you the one who was to come, or should we expect someone else?' Good though the reports were that he had received, there wasn't much evidence of fire, judgment and the burning up of chaff spoken of so confidently in Luke chapter 3. It was John after all who had confronted Herod and landed in prison for his efforts, while Jesus was still free to wander about, gaining popularity!

The Lord's reply was fascinating. Quoting two well-known Messianic passages from the book of Isaiah 35:5 and 61:1, Jesus indicated He had indeed come to fulfill expectations of Messiahship but what John (along with Jesus' own disciples, including Peter) did not fully understand at that time was that Messiahship would entail Jesus Himself taking on the fire of God's judgment and punishment and death. He was indeed Messiah, but not as John envisaged it, and so Jesus urged patience.

Things are not always straightforward. God's ways are not always our ways, nor His thoughts ours. We don't necessarily understand everything there is to know about God or His methods. Painful and puzzling though it may be for a while, keep on keeping on. Don't give up. Refuse to despair. God is still in control.

QUESTION

Is there something I can't yet fully understand but about which I just need to trust God right now?

PRAYER

'Courage Christian, do not stumble though your path be dark as night.

There's a star to guide the humble. Trust in God and do the right.

Let the road be rough and dreary and its end far out of sight.

Foot it bravely, strong or weary. Trust in God and do the right.'[1]

---

1. 'Courage Christian'. Norman MacLeod 1857 (1812-1872).

'What did you go to see?'

After John's messengers left, Jesus began to speak to the crowd about Him.

Just as John had borne witness to Jesus, so now Jesus bore witness to John and in spite of the baptiser's momentary doubts, defended John's godly reputation.

'What did you go out into the wilderness to see? A reed swayed by the wind? A man dressed in fine clothes? No, those who wear expensive clothes and indulge in luxury are in palaces. But who did you go out to see? A prophet? Yes, I tell you, and more than a prophet!'

Some historians contend that there is a direct and deliberate comparison of John the Baptist incarcerated in Herod's prison with Tetrarch Antipas who had put him there. Some of the coins that Antipas minted featured a bent reed surrounding Herod's name and portrait. When the people went out into the desert to see John, was it to be impressed by some crooked stalk? A weak, immoral, easily swayed ruler?

Had they gone to all that effort simply to view a man like Herod with a liking for strutting around in fine attire?

Not at all!

When the people had crowded to see John, it wasn't to fawn over trumped up minor royalty but to hear a message from John about the King of Kings and the Lord of Lords!

As forerunner of Messiah, John had not only spoken the Word of God fulfilling a role of far greater importance than any privileged person parading pomp and power, but uniquely, John had also been spoken about in the Word of God.

The Scriptures had anticipated him in the Old Testament prophesy of Malachi.

'Let me lay it out for you as plainly as I can,' said Jesus 'No one in history surpasses John the Baptiser' (Luke 7:28, MSG).

Whatever great person you can think of in the Hebrew Scriptures: Abraham, Moses, David or Isaiah, none is greater: for John, unprecedently of all these greats, was sent by God, to physically point out Messiah!

QUESTION

Am I being unduly influenced by entertainment and social media into thinking money, leisure and fame are the way to fulfilment?

PRAYER

Heavenly Father, I can so easily be impressed by celebrity and people of wealth and power. Give me eyes to see true greatness and to honour those who bring glory to you. For Jesus' sake. Amen.

The Pharisees' and Sadducees' response

Many, many people – even the despised tax collectors – sensed deep within their spirits that Jesus' praise of John was merited. Unpalatable and not very politically correct though his message may have been, they knew what he said was true (v. 29).

Not all shared this opinion, however. The Scribes and Pharisees in particular refused to acknowledge that what John had to say was applicable to them!

As men who prided themselves on meritoriously keeping every element of the law, they did not consider themselves 'sinners' and relied on their own good efforts to gain status before God.

They felt certain that when it came to judgment day, God, like a kindly headmaster, would overlook any minor shortcomings they may have displayed and give them a gold star for effort.

They regarded John with supercilious disdain and disregarded his coarse and unconventional ways as illustration of his oddity. Calling John 'demonic' enabled them to dismiss him and his uncomfortable words.

Elsewhere Jesus described this sort of twisted behaviour as the unforgivable sin (Mark 3:28-30): attributing to the Holy Spirit what is evil and dismissing truth by labelling it 'bad'. There is nothing more perverse than this and it is hugely prevalent today, demanding people call good, 'wicked' and disgrace, 'natural'.

'John the Baptist came neither eating bread nor drinking wine, and you say, "He has a demon." The Son of Man came eating and drinking, and you say, "Here is a glutton and a drunkard, a friend of tax collectors and sinners."'

In other words, the believer can't win! If someone rejects a person for their integrity, truthfulness and godliness then no matter what they do, it will not be sufficient to cause that other person to change their minds. They will continue to reject the messenger as well as the message.

But actually, the believer will be vindicated at the end.

Because, as Jesus concludes, 'Wisdom is proved right by all her children' (Luke 7:35). Even as a good tree produces good fruit so the way of righteousness will eventually become abundantly evident for all to see.

QUESTION
Have I become dulled to recognise bad from good and lulled into believing holiness is no longer important?

PRAYER
Gracious God, there are many pressures in society to condone things you call evil as 'good' and to be embarrassed by godly behaviour as intolerant and outdated. Help me to keep my head and be more concerned with what you think than what people think of me, and this I pray for Jesus' sake. Amen.

'He has a demon'

'John the Baptist came neither eating bread nor drinking wine, and you say, "He has a demon." The Son of Man came eating and drinking and you say, "Here is a glutton and a drunkard, a friend of tax collectors and sinners."'

As an aesthetic and a Nazirite, John had been set aside from birth as a teetotaler.

As someone dedicated to the service of God, John chose to live simply, rejecting ordinary earthly 'necessities' in order to focus his attention on his heavenly calling.

Jesus too had been set aside from His earliest days, dedicated to God and His service, but that did not prevent Him from partaking in everyday food and wine.

Which was wrong and which was right?

As far as the religious leaders of the day were concerned, neither was right!

John was wrong because his aestheticism made him stand out like a sore thumb and look odd socially. Jesus was wrong because His choice of spending time with dishonorable kinds of people made Him look as if He was no different from 'sinners'.

But actually, as fellow believers who sought to honour God, both were right!

John was right because he remained faithful to his calling, and in his short time on earth encouraged people to get ready to meet their maker. Jesus was right because out of an open and transparent relationship with His loving Heavenly Father, He fulfilled His chief responsibility: 'I have not come to call the righteous, but sinners to repentance' (Luke 5:32).

QUESTION
How can I live in such a way that puts Jesus first in all my choices?

PRAYER
Heavenly Father, it's difficult living as a Christian in a post-Christian society. Grant me wisdom to know how best to navigate tricky social situations with both integrity and grace. Amen.

John arrested by Herod

L ife is hard. Following Jesus doesn't necessarily make it easier.

Near the start of Jesus' life Matthew began his Gospel with a story about Herod (Matt. 2). It was Herod 'the Great' who attempted to kill the infant Jesus, after wise men from the East came to Jerusalem seeking to worship the one born 'King of the Jews'. Tolerating no rival, Herod alone coveted that ascription.

Now again, near the start of Jesus' adult ministry we meet another Herod: Herod Antipas, son of Herod the Great. This Herod arrested, bound and put into prison John the Baptist who had had the temerity to point out Herod's immoral behaviour, rendering him wholly ineligible to be the legitimate 'King of the Jews'.

At the end of Luke's Gospel there is a third mention of Herod (Luke 23). It is no more glorious than the other two. Pontius Pilate, the Roman Governor, sent Jesus to Herod for trial on hearing that Jesus was a Galilean and therefore under Herod's jurisdiction. While initially pleased to meet Jesus, as he hoped to see Him perform a miracle, Jesus remained silent in the face of Herod's arrogant questioning, mocking and ridiculing before being returned to Pilate for crucifixion, with the sign emblazoned above His head: 'This is the King of the Jews' (Luke 23:38).

Here was true royalty. Christ's kingship placarded in jest to the world, yet profoundly true. Jesus reigning from a cross, soon to be enthroned in heaven and granting a place of honour, not to the proud, but to the truly repentant (Luke 23:43).

QUESTION
Do I secretly imagine that being a Christian is supposed to make my life easier?

PRAYER
Dear God, thank you for the Lord Jesus, the authentic King, creator of the universe, sustainer of the world and Lord of the Church. Enable me to bow before Him with adoration, humility, and wonder and enable me to worship with a life of obedience, love and praise. Amen.

Herod's birthday bash

On Herod's birthday he held a party to which lots of guests were invited for dinner – lavish food and drink and a full programme of glittering entertainment.

Having fallen for Herodius, who was at the time his brother's wife, Antipas's eye was now captured by the dancing of his stepdaughter Salome.

Rash Herod made a promise greater than sober sense. Just like foolish King Belshazzar in Daniel chapter 5, drunk with pride and alcohol, the Apostle Mark adds that Herod swore to Salome: 'Whatever you ask I will give you, up to half my kingdom' (Mark 6:23).

What might a young lady like when offered such a generous thing? Designer clothes? Sparkling jewellery? A city shopping spree to Rome?

Salome turned to her mother for advice and that bitter, vengeful woman replied, 'The head of John the Baptist.'

Having himself been off his head with drink, Herod now considered the sobering implications of his proud boast; but the rashness of his words and his inability to repent led to the gruesome and unjustifiable murder of the teetotal and godly John.

A year older but none the wiser, Herod had John executed at his birthday bash and, in stark contrast to the shocking disrespect displayed to him, John's disciples came and lovingly cared for his body.

There is one other little sentence in this sad story which can easily be overlooked. Having experienced this horrible bereavement, Matthew tells us, 'Then John's disciples went and told Jesus.' Today there are many similarly shocking stories of suffering, death and martyrdom: followers of Jesus Christ in various parts of the world unjustly imprisoned, cruelly treated and even beheaded for their faith. What is the first and right thing to do when such unspeakable things take place? Tell Jesus. According to Matthew 14:12 that's appropriate. In fact, that's the very best thing to do.

QUESTION

Is there a deep-seated concern that I need to share with Jesus right now?

PRAYER

Gracious God, there is so much trouble in this world and so many of our brothers and sisters are suffering for their faith. Before I despair or wonder what I can best do to help, enable me to cast all my anxieties on Jesus, knowing that He cares for me. Amen.

Jesus' reaction to John's death

When Jesus heard what had happened, He withdrew to a solitary place by boat. Jesus needed time out to think, rest and pray.

His peace and tranquility didn't last long because 14:14 tells us large crowds followed Him and, having compassion on them, He healed the sick.

Jesus' reaction to John's death was to find space, but when He was interrupted, never to take His anger, grief or frustration out on those who were in need or unaware of His personal sorrow.

In total contrast to the proud, self-centred, boastful and out-of-control Herod, Jesus the true King of the Jews dealt kindly with His subjects and exercised authentic authority by speaking words of healing to the sick and words of calm to the troubled elements, 'Don't be afraid!' (Matt. 14:27).

Around that time (v. 1), Herod heard reports about Jesus, and said to his attendants, 'This is John the Baptist: he has risen from the dead!'

In a strange moment of stricken conscience, like the guilt-ridden Lady Macbeth, Herod imagined John had come back to haunt him.

Jesus' marvellous deeds do indeed point to the resurrection, not because they are a result of it but because they anticipate it. Transformation and peace come not through the resurrection of John, but Christ!

QUESTION

In times of personal sorrow and grief how might I draw from Christ's deep well of resourcefulness?

PRAYER

'King of the ages, Almighty God,
Perfect love, ever just and true.
Who will not fear You and bring You praise?
All the nations will come to You.
The day will come when You appear,
And every eye shall see You.
Then we shall rise with hearts ablaze,
With a song we will sing forever. Amen.'
(Keith Getty and Stuart Townend, 2002)

'John baptised with water ... you will be baptised with the Holy Spirit'

If the Gospel of Luke is the story of what Jesus started to do leading up to and including the cross, resurrection and ascension, the Book of Acts is what Jesus continued to do after Pentecost. 'John baptised with water, but in a few days you will be baptised with the Holy Spirit' (1:5).

This event was the one John the Baptist had foretold in Luke 3:16 when people wondered if he might possibly be the Christ. John's ministry was powerful. He was the last and greatest of all the Old Testament prophets, but his baptism was a pre-Christian washing, pointing to the one who would baptise with the Holy Spirit.

Now John had fulfilled his responsibilities. The spotlight had turned away from Jordan toward Jerusalem, from the old covenant to the new and from this Elijah-type figure to the ultimate Prophet, Priest and King combined – Jesus Christ, Son of God, Messiah.

Jesus would do what only the one who operates with the Father's authority could do; grant extraordinary supernatural power for Christ-exalting ministry. Enabling ordinary, fragile, disciples to be empowered to do what no human being could ever do even by their own well-intentioned self-determination: to be Jesus' witnesses in Jerusalem and Judea and Samaria and to the ends of the earth.

And this is precisely what happened! When the Day of Pentecost arrived, what sounded like the blowing of a violent wind came, and what seemed like tongues of fire rested on the believers and they began to speak in languages other than their own, proclaiming the meaning of the cross, resurrection and ascension to peoples from all over the then-known world. The Holy Spirit enabled the confusion of Babel to be reversed (Gen. 11) and the promise of Genesis 12:3 to be fulfilled – that through Abraham's seed, all peoples on earth would be blessed!

QUESTION

In what way might I draw on the Holy Spirit's supernatural resources to witness in a way that can be easily understood by someone today?

PRAYER

'Grace unmeasured, vast and free
That knew me from eternity
That called me out before my birth
To bring You glory on this earth
Grace amazing, pure and deep
That saw me in my misery
That took my curse and owned my blame
So I could bear Your righteous name.
    Grace paid for my sins
    And brought me to life
    Grace clothes me with power
    To do what is right.'
(Bob Kauflin, Sovereign Grace Music, 2005)

John's baptism and Christian baptism

Some years after Jesus' resurrection and ascension to heaven, the Apostle Paul was on a visit to the Greek city of Ephesus.

'There he found some disciples and asked them, "Did you receive the Holy Spirit when you believed?"

They answered, "No, we have not even heard that there is a Holy Spirit."

So Paul asked, "Then what baptism did you receive?"

"John's baptism," they replied.

Paul said, "John's baptism was a baptism of repentance. He told the people to believe in the one coming after him, that is, in Jesus"' (Acts 19:1-4).

On hearing this, they received Christian baptism. John's baptism was an outward symbol of repentance indicating a person's desire to renounce sin and serve God. That was good. Christian baptism is even better. It is less about us and more about Jesus and what He has done for us on the cross.

When Paul discovered these disciples in Ephesus had not heard of the Holy Spirit, he baptised them in the name of the Lord Jesus. Names are significant (as Zechariah found out!). Being baptised in Jesus' name means being baptised into Him (Acts 3:6, Acts 4:22). Under Christ's authority and in His name, the Holy Spirit came upon these believers with evidences of His presence and power.

In the succinct words of The Westminster Larger Catechism Question 165:

'Baptism is a sign and seal of in-grafting into Christ, of remission of sins by his blood, and regeneration by his Spirit; of adoption, and resurrection unto everlasting life; whereby the parties baptised are solemnly admitted into the visible church, and enter into an open and professed engagement to be wholly and only the Lord's.'

On hearing the gospel being preached by the Apostle Peter on the Day of Pentecost (about twenty years before Paul's visit to Ephesus), the people were cut to the heart and asked, 'What shall we do?' Peter replied, 'Repent and be baptised, every one of you, in the name of Jesus Christ for the forgiveness of your sins. And you will receive the gift of the Holy Spirit. The promise is for you and your children and for all who are far off—for all whom the Lord our God will call' (Acts 2:38-39).

QUESTION

If I am a Christian and have never been baptised, why not? If I am a follower of the Lord Jesus and have been baptised either early in life or in adulthood, am I appreciative of the enormous privileges and responsibilities that come with this sign and seal of God's unmerited grace and incorporated as part of the worldwide people of God?

PRAYER

In many places today baptism in Jesus' name is tantamount to a death sentence. I pray for all for whom it is enormously costly to believe.

Teach me, good Lord, to serve you as you deserve. To give and not to count the cost. To fight and not to heed the wounds. To toil and not to seek for rest. To labour and not to ask for any reward, save that of knowing that I do your will. In Jesus' most glorious name. Amen.

Conclusion

Perhaps through this consideration of the Bible texts we have gained a little insight into why, from Jesus' perspective, the one who had gone before was not just a 'good' man ... not even a 'great' person, but 'the greatest who ever existed'. John the Baptist hadn't just appeared 'out of the blue'. As the forerunner of Messiah, the Hebrew Scriptures make reference to him in both Isaiah 40: 3-5 and in Malachi chapters 3 and 4.

But though we have been studying John the Baptist, I wonder if you have noticed, we have actually been thinking a great deal more about Jesus than John!

There is not one day over the past month that John hasn't pointed away from himself and helped us to fix our gaze on Christ. But then, that was his wish.

That was his number-one goal and calling.

John's greatness lay in Jesus' personal affirmation of him and the office he fulfilled: as prophet of the Most High God.

John's greatness lay in the message he proclaimed: repentance from sin and a turning toward the Lord.

John's greatness lay in the humility he epitomised: his integrity, sincerity, life and witness to God.

John's greatness lay in the fact that, uniquely of all Bible prophets, John bore first-hand witness to Jesus Christ as the Son of the Living God.

But John said, 'I am not.'

Instead he pointed people to the one who said:

I AM the Bread of Life.

I AM the Light of the world.

I AM the Door.

I AM the Good Shepherd.

I AM the Resurrection and the Life.

I AM the Way, the Truth and the Life.

I AM the Vine.

John was great because he pointed people to the great I AM!

Yet astonishingly, incredibly, Jesus continued what He said in Matthew 11:11 with some more words that are even more startling.

Jesus concluded by saying, 'Yet, the person who is least in the Kingdom of Heaven is greater than he!'

Disciples of Jesus: believing women and men, boys and girls who are part of the Kingdom Jesus has inaugurated, are not 'better than' John but have 'even more privileges' than the Baptiser. How?

John preached to the people of Israel (Acts 13:24).

Christ's Spirit-filled disciples are commissioned to go into all the whole-wide world to proclaim the gospel (Matt. 28:18-20).

John preached the necessity of repentance (Luke 3:3).

Christ's repentant disciples know and proclaim the joys of full redemption (Eph. 1:3-14).

John expounded the law, requiring obedience and the way of righteousness (Matt. 21:32).

Christ's disciples experience the fulfilment of Jeremiah 31:31-34 where, under the new covenant, God places His law within minds and writes it on hearts.

John was filled with the Holy Spirit for a particular purpose (Luke 1:15).

Christ's disciples are drenched by the Spirit of Truth for 'He lives with you and will be in you' (John 14:17).

John had the opportunity of pointing to Jesus the sacrificial Lamb in His first coming (John 1:29).

Christ's disciples, having benefited from His atoning death and resurrection of the Lord Jesus (Rom. 4:25) have now the even greater privilege of pointing people to Christ the living, reigning Lamb who will come again in glory (Rev. 5:6-14).

'And the angels will cry:
"Hail the Lamb who was slain for the world.
Rule in power!"
And the earth will reply:
"You shall reign
As the King of all kings
And the LORD of all lords."'[1]

---

1. 'Lion of Judah', Robin Mark, 1999.

The Christian's greatness then lies not in anything we have done but in the fullness of His grace which we have received through Him (John 1:16).

For mistakes we can't forget
and the sins that still beset...
We have a Lamb.
For our fraught and anxious realm,
for the fears that overwhelm...
We have a throne.

We sing worthy, worthy is the Lamb
Who was slain for the world —
Royal arms unfurled.
We sing glory, glory to the Christ:
Your cross — our Fountain of Life.

For our lost and lonely hearts,
for our gnarled and tangled paths...
We have a Shepherd.
For our dry and listless souls
and our thirst for being whole...
We have a Stream.

We sing worthy, worthy is the Lamb
Who was slain for the world —
Royal arms unfurled.
We sing glory, glory to the Christ:
Your cross — our Fountain of Life.

For regret and ravaged years,
for all sweet and bitter tears...
We have a Father.
For our treks through burning sands,
To our home in promised lands,
This hope till all is done:
Our God the three-in-one.

We sing worthy, worthy is the Lamb
Who was slain for the world —
Royal arms unfurled.
We sing glory, glory to the Christ:
Your cross — our Fountain of Life.[2]

---

2. 'We have a lamb', written by Glen Scrivener and put to music by Phil Moore (2020).

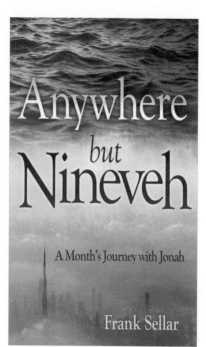

Anywhere
but
Nineveh

A Month's Journey with Jonah

Frank Sellar

Anywhere But Nineveh
A Month's Journey with Jonah
Frank Sellar

So often, just like Jonah, we are blinded by our situations, culture, or our own hearts. So often we ignore what we know God is calling us to do – and we are always left feeling incomplete and far from Him.

Anywhere but Nineveh is a thirty day devotional which inspires and focuses the mind, not on our rebellion, but instead on a God who speaks to us and on "One greater than Jonah" Who did not run away.

In all of his phases, Frank Sellar has been consistent - a man sold out for the good news of Jesus, committed to encouraging any form of positive ministry to the weird and wonderful thing that is church, and someone whose generosity and encouragement always leaves us thankful for the encounter.

I know reading this book will do the same for you.

Keith Getty
Hymn-writer

ISBN 978-1-7819-1862-3

From Glory to Golgotha

CONTROVERSIAL ISSUES
IN THE LIFE OF CHRIST

DONALD MACLEOD

From Glory to Golgotha
Controversial Issues in the Life of Christ
Donald Macleod

Renowned theologian and author, Donald Macleod explains controversial topics from the life of Christ with clarity and care. Staying true to the biblical text he points readers to reflect on the Saviour who has captivated his own heart and mind. This new edition includes 4 new chapters, originally published as articles on the Desiring God website.

... passion and intensity, decades of study, deep theological reflection and serious polemical interaction, and even more, the heart of a believing theologian who knows he needs Christ and His Cross. If your prayer is 'more love to Thee, O Christ,' here is fuel for your devotion. Read and believe and worship.

Ligon Duncan
Chancellor and CEO, Reformed Theological Seminary

ISBN 978-1-5271-0636-9

IT WILL

COST

YOU

EVERY
THING

WHAT IT TAKES TO FOLLOW JESUS

STEVEN J. LAWSON

It Will Cost You Everything
What it Takes to Follow Jesus
Steven J. Lawson

Nestled in a few verses in Luke's Gospel is a Jesus who would not have been tolerated today: He was not politically correct and He certainly did not try to save people's feelings. Steven Lawson unpacks these few verses, looking at the unashamed honesty, passion, and urgency with which Jesus explains the life–long cost involved in choosing to follow Him. True Christianity is the biggest sacrifice any person ever makes ... but it is in pursuit of the most precious prize ever glimpsed.

This book is a 'must-read' for all! The unconverted will hear the gospel; the Christian will find the true road to devotion and joy....

Paul Washer
Founder and Missions Director, Heart Cry Ministry,
Radford, Virginia

Like a master builder Steve Lawson gives us the foundation of Jesus' own words to erect a frame showing the cost, demands, gains and losses of following Christ. In doing so, Dr. Lawson gives us a strong and firm edifice that brings glory to Him and His truth.

R. C. Sproul, (1939 – 2017)
Founder & Chairman of Ligonier Ministries, Orlando,
Florida

ISBN 978-1-5271-0703-8